Musical Instruments

Piano

By Nick Rebman

level 1 little blue readers

www.littlebluehousebooks.com

Copyright © 2023 by Little Blue House, Mendota Heights, MN 55120. All rights reserved. No part of this book may be reproduced or utilized in any form or by any means without written permission from the publisher.

Little Blue House is distributed by North Star Editions:
sales@northstareditions.com | 888-417-0195

Produced for Little Blue House by Red Line Editorial.

Photographs ©: Shutterstock Images, cover, 4, 7, 8–9, 10–11, 12–13, 15, 16–17, 19, 21, 24 (top left), 24 (top right), 24 (bottom left), 24 (bottom right); iStockphoto, 22–23

Library of Congress Control Number: 2022910596

ISBN
978-1-64619-700-2 (hardcover)
978-1-64619-732-3 (paperback)
978-1-64619-793-4 (ebook pdf)
978-1-64619-764-4 (hosted ebook)

Printed in the United States of America
Mankato, MN
012023

About the Author

Nick Rebman is a writer and editor who lives in Minnesota. He enjoys reading, walking his dog, and playing rock songs on his drum set.

Table of Contents

Piano **5**

Glossary **24**

Index **24**

Piano

I like to make music.

I play the piano.

I sit on a bench.

I keep my back straight.

The piano has 88 keys.

Some keys are white.

Some keys are black.

I put my hands on the keys.

I press a key.

Each key plays a different note.

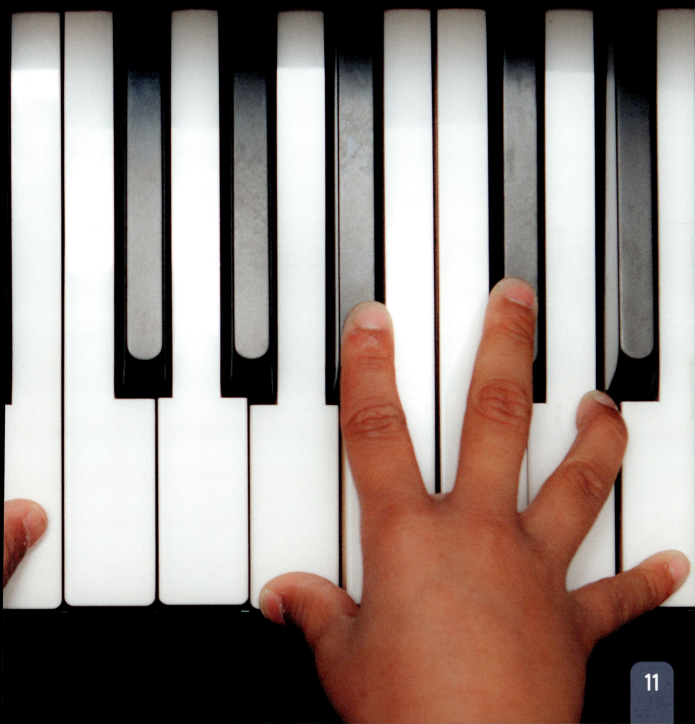

The piano has pedals.

I push them with my feet.

The pedals change how the notes sound.

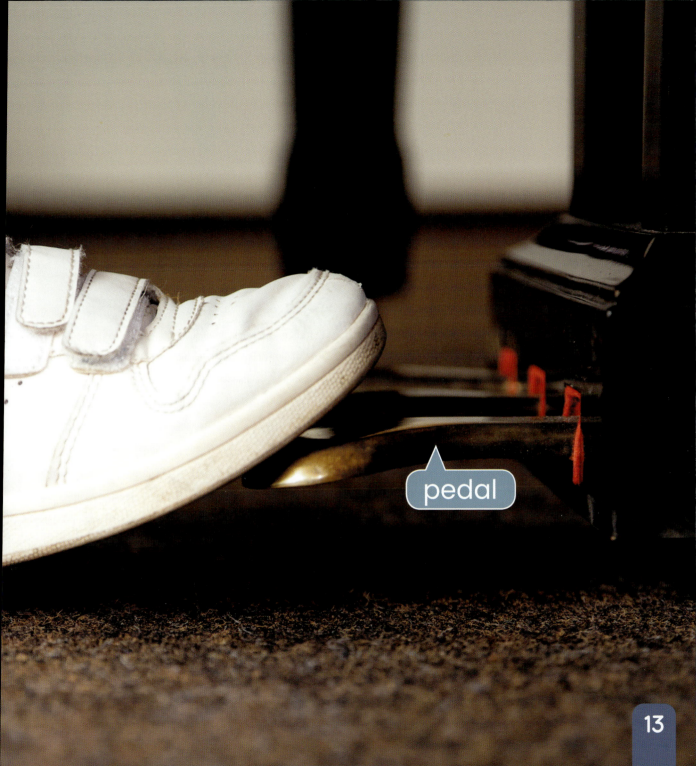

I sit next to my teacher.

She shows me how

to play.

I learn how to read sheet music.

I play slowly at first.

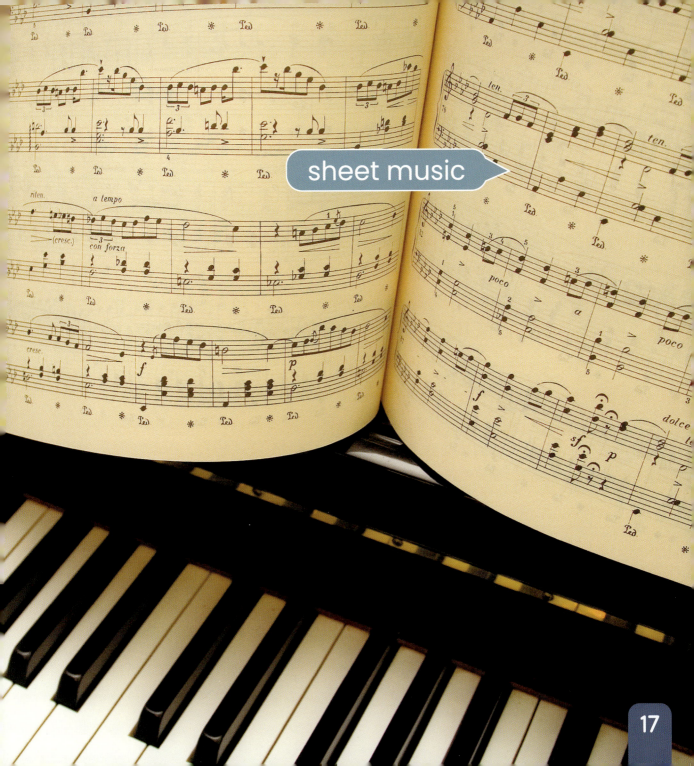

I practice every day.

I get better and better.

Soon I can play faster.

I play for other people.

The piano is on a stage.

stage

I play with friends.

We have fun

making music.

Glossary

keys

sheet music

pedals

stage

Index

B
bench, 6

F
friends, 22

N
notes, 10, 12

P
practice, 18